SPACE SHUTTLES
A NEW ERA?

© Aladdin Books 1989

Designed and produced by
Aladdin Books Ltd
70 Old Compton Street
London W1

*First published in the
United States in 1989 by*
Gloucester Press
387 Park Avenue South
New York, NY 10016

Design: Rob Hillier
Editor: Margaret Fagan
Researcher: Cecilia Weston-Baker

ISBN 0-531-17139-6

Library of Congress Catalog
Card Number: 88-83097

Printed in Belgium

The front cover photograph shows the launch of Discovery,
September 29, 1988.
The back cover shows the first photograph of the Soviet shuttle.

The author, Nigel Hawkes, was formerly science correspondent of
The Observer *newspaper, London, and has written several children's
books on space. Today he is diplomatic correspondent of* The Observer.

*The consultant, Dr. John Becklake, is head of the Department of
Engineering, Science Museum, London.*

Contents

SPACE SHUTTLES
A NEW ERA?

NIGEL HAWKES

Illustrated by
Ron Hayward Associates

Gloucester Press
New York : London : Toronto : Sydney

Back in business

There were cheers, tears and audible sighs of relief from a crowd of 250,000 when the United States space shuttle Discovery lifted off from the pad at Cape Kennedy on September 29, 1988. Two and a half years before, Discovery's sister ship, Challenger, had blown up there, killing all seven aboard. Another disaster would have destroyed the American space program.

Five thousand miles away, in Moscow, the Russians were also watching the launch. They chose that day to release the first pictures of their own shuttle, which looked very similar to the American design.

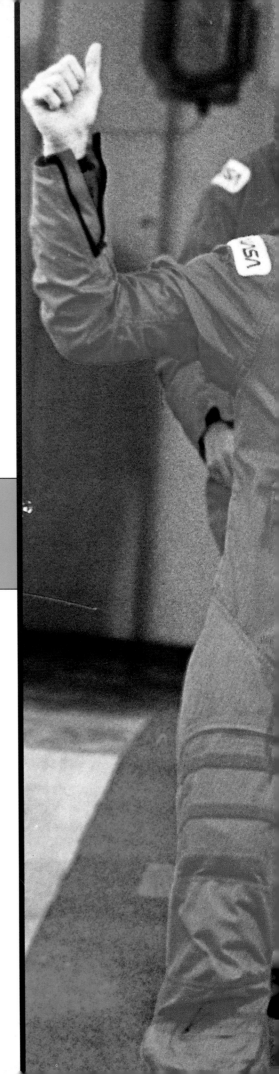

▷ Pilot Dick Covey (left) and Commander Frederick Hauck lead other members of the Discovery crew on board the shuttle before a flawless launch and successful flight proved that the United States was back in space.

The Soviet shuttle, named Buran, was successfully launched on November 15, 1988. Its first flight was unmanned and controlled throughout from Earth.

Why have both superpowers developed shuttles so similar in shape and size? With them, humans can start building the first large-scale colonies in space, permanently manned bases from which to launch expeditions to the planets and beyond some time in the next century.

Like much else in the modern world, the two shuttles are the product of superpower rivalry. Will shuttles carry that rivalry into space and be used to build battle stations there to dominate man's last frontier? Or will they make possible a new era of cooperation in space? This book will try to find some answers.

4

Shuttles in space

The United States designed its shuttle as a cheaper way of getting into space. It was hoped that by reusing the same vehicle, costs would be cut and space travel would be transformed.

Yet the National Aeronautics and Space Administration (NASA) has found that it takes much longer than expected to turn the shuttle around after each mission and get it ready to launch again. The number of launches is much smaller than was hoped, and the cost of each mission is high – over $200 million, no cheaper than a conventional "throwaway" rocket. The Challenger disaster also hurt the US shuttle's credibility, enabling the European Space Agency's (ESA) rocket to win launch contracts.

By the late 1990s the United States shuttle will find its proper role: ferrying astronauts and materials to and from a permanent space station in Earth's orbit. Sections of the space station will be carried up one by one and assembled along spines which form the skeleton of the space station. The picture shows an artist's impression of a NASA space station.

So why are both superpowers continuing to develop shuttles? First of all, even if shuttles are not the best way of getting things up into space, they are the *only* way of getting them down. No other vehicle can recapture expensive satellites and bring them back for servicing. Secondly a space station will need a shuttle to supply it with crews and raw materials, and to take its products back to Earth. Eventually the shuttle could function as a space "van."

Ultimately, it is still hoped that a reusable vehicle will be cheaper to operate. The first shuttles were prototypes. The next generation of shuttles will be more reliable and may achieve what the first have failed to do.

Manned space flight
The US space program has always favored manned missions. The reusable shuttle was designed for ferrying people to and from space stations. But since the Challenger disaster, NASA is planning more automated shuttle flight.

Unmanned space flight
The Russians claim that their shuttle is safer than the American shuttle because it can be remote controlled. They will make a manned flight only when the shuttle's systems have been tested in automated flight.

Advantages of shuttles:
1. In principle, they are cheaper to operate, given a quick turnaround and enough flights per year.
2. They can fetch as well as carry, bringing down large payloads from orbit for repair or servicing.
3. Shuttles land on runways like aircraft, simpler and safer than parachuting into the sea like older space capsules.
4. Shuttles are designed to be long-lasting and were once regarded as tough work horses, but since Challenger they are recognized as fragile craft.

Advantages of rockets:
1. Less complex, because they only need to work once, not repeatedly.
2. Much cheaper for launching small unmanned satellites, because, unlike the shuttles, they do not need all the equipment to support life in space.
3. Familiar, proven technology which at present provides a better guarantee of getting a commercial satellite into orbit on time.
4. Rockets are easier to launch; the Russians send up two rockets a week without elaborate preparations.

◁ Enterprise was the first of the shuttles. It was used for landing tests and never actually flew in space.

Setback

Few people who saw it can forget the moment when Challenger blew up, etching brilliant yellow traces against the blue sky. It was the 25th flight of a vehicle that despite some problems had worked well, carrying 126 astronauts into space and launching 28 satellites.

One of the two powerful solid fuel boosters had sprung a leak at a point where two sections of the casing joined together. A tongue of escaping flame burned through the main tank and ignited the fuel, blowing the vehicle apart. The design of the joint was poor, and exceptionally cold weather had prevented the "O-ring" from sealing shut.

▽ The successful launch of Discovery assured the future of the US manned space program. NASA has scheduled 50 shuttle flights in the next five years.

The two solid fuel boosters flew off in different directions after the Challenger explosion. The crew compartment remained intact until it hit the sea but the crew had no means of bailing out even if they survived the explosion.

Since then, a big program of improvements has been carried out by NASA. The failed joint has been redesigned and changes have also been made to the main rocket motors and the undercarriage. Hundreds of smaller changes have been made to try to ensure safety.

But the biggest change is one of attitude. NASA will think twice before sending ordinary people, like teacher Christa McAuliffe, into space again. The shuttle is a prototype, unsuitable for joyriding. NASA always expected one major failure every 50 flights or so – the Challenger disaster simply came a little sooner than they had anticipated.

▽ Major changes were made to Discovery to increase safety. They included: (1) new computers to replace older 1960s models (2) an explosive hatch to enable the crew to eject in an emergency (3) better brakes to replace those that had burned through on earlier landings (4) new engine fuel valves and (5) most important of all, the joint that leaked was replaced with a safer one.

A fresh start

Discovery's mission lasted only four days and had modest objectives. The astronauts released a relay satellite that will be used to keep in touch with future shuttle flights. They made a few scientific observations, held a press conference in space, then landed safely in California.

Future missions will be more ambitious. The shuttle will launch the Hubble space telescope, an 11 ton, $1.2 billion instrument with ten times the resolution of any ground-based telescope. This will enable astronomers to probe deeper into space, seeing objects seven times further away than anyone has seen before. The shuttle will visit the telescope regularly during its 20-year life, even bringing it back to Earth for repair if necessary.

The shuttle will also carry into orbit the Galileo spacecraft, designed to carry out an unmanned exploration of the planet Jupiter and its moons. Now that the US shuttle program is safely established again, it is expected that shuttle flights will take place every few months.

△ Discovery glides in and makes a perfect touchdown at Edwards Air Force Base in the Mohave Desert, California. It was the 26th shuttle launch – and almost trouble-free.

Space research
The main task of the Discovery mission was to launch a Tracking and Data Relay Satellite (TDRS). Because shuttles fly in low orbits, they would be out of direct touch with ground control for long periods without the TDRS satellites, which relay messages. The astronauts also studied the influence of weightlessness on red blood cells and crystals.

The zero-gravity of space is ideal for purifying biological materials. Future missions will manufacture drugs like urokinase (for treating heart disease), interferon (a possible cancer drug) and human hormones that are almost impossible to make on Earth. Scientists are also hoping that experiments carried out in space may help to find the urgently needed vaccine against AIDS.

▽ The Galileo spacecraft, after release by the shuttle, will journey to Jupiter.

▷ The Hubble telescope is the largest and most expensive scientific spacecraft ever assembled.

A home in space

By 1994, the United States aims to have a permanently manned space station (Freedom) in orbit around the Earth, assembled from pieces carried up by the shuttle. Here people will live and work in zero-gravity, carrying out scientific experiments, manufacturing products, and servicing and repairing satellites. The European Space Agency, Canada and Japan will also contribute to the operation and production.

▽ The space station living and working areas — the cylindrical capsules — will be carried up by the shuttle and attached to a light framework. Power will come from large arrays of solar cells.

Twenty shuttle missions are planned to carry the modules from which the station will be built. The modules have been designed to fit into the shuttle's cargo bay. Some modules will be used for living quarters while others will be work spaces. All will be filled with air at normal pressure and provided with electrical power from a huge array of solar cells. There will be eight crew members, each serving a three-month tour of duty before being replaced by fresh crew members sent up in the shuttle.

Skylab was the first US laboratory to be taken up in space — a forerunner of space stations. It was launched on May 14, 1973 and was manned by three separate crews of three astronauts for a total of 171 days. It was the first full-scale observatory in space.

△ Spacelab, built by ESA, fitted into the shuttle's cargo bay. It consisted of a pressurized laboratory in which the scientists worked, and an open platform, exposed to space, on which instruments like a telescope were placed. It made four flights between November 1983 and October 1985 and carried out numerous scientific experiments and observations.

Crew members will have many jobs. The space station will be a laboratory, an observatory for gazing into space or down at the Earth, a garage for assembling, repairing or servicing satellites, and a plant for manufacturing exotic alloys and valuable drugs. Operations in space, NASA declares, have become vital for science, technology and national security – and a space station is needed as a base from which to carry them out.

▽ Astronauts have floated free to capture satellites and carried out repairs in the shuttle payload bay.

Soviet plans

On May 15, 1987 the Soviet Union took a decisive step towards launching its own shuttle and building the first large-scale settlement in space. It was the first flight of a massive new booster rocket, called Energia, which can carry up to 100 tons into Earth orbit or send a 30-ton spacecraft to the Moon or Mars.

Energia is almost 200 feet tall, with four liquid-fueled rocket motors. Around the central core can be strapped up to 6 boosters, also liquid fueled. With four strap-ons, as in the first flight, Energia's thrust is about the same as the now-discontinued Saturn 5 which took the Apollo spacecraft to the Moon, and five times more powerful than any previous Soviet launcher.

Earlier Soviet attempts to build a heavy booster ended in disaster after a huge explosion on the pad in 1969 demolished one rocket, and a second shook itself to pieces in 1972 at an altitude of only 7 miles (11 km). The Energia launch in 1987 was not completely successful – the third stage engine failed to work – but it went far better than earlier attempts.

Energia's job is to lift the Soviet shuttle, which has no rocket motors of its own, carry up huge components which can be used to build a space city and launch manned missions to the Moon or the planets. The US shuttle's payload is 30 tons – a fraction of what Energia can lift – and American planners are now thinking again about designing a heavy booster of their own.

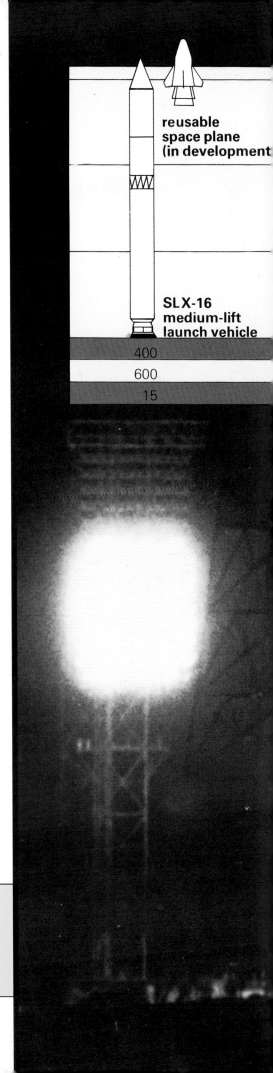

reusable
space plane
(in development

SLX-16
medium-lift
launch vehicle

400

600

15

▷ Energia, one of the most powerful rockets ever built, was launched for the first time at night. Its power damaged the launch pad severely, and its satellite failed to get into orbit, but the launch was declared a great success.

14

197 ft (60m)

131 ft (40m)

66 ft (20m)

**SL-W
shuttle**

**SL-W
heavy-lift
launch vehicle**

◁ The Soviet Union has two new launchers in development: Energia, which can lift the shuttle or other heavy payloads, and the SLX-16, a medium-thrust rocket capable of putting 15-ton satellites into low orbits. It will launch a small Soviet spaceplane called Kosmolyet in the 1990s.

2,000	2,000	Lift-off weight
3,000	3,000	Lift-off thrust
30	100	Payload to 112km (180 miles)

eights in tons

The Soviet shuttle

▽ The first picture of the Soviet shuttle on the launch pad showed how it is similar to the US one – a result, NASA claims, of highly successful industrial espionage. A huge crawler (bottom right) carried Energia and the shuttle Buran to the Baikonur launch pad ready for take off.

Over the years the Russians have criticized the United States' shuttle program and denied that they were developing a shuttle of their own. But as Discovery went into space, the Russians released pictures of their own shuttle which had been developed in the utmost secrecy. On November 15, 1988, this shuttle lifted off from Baikonur Cosmodrome in Siberia. The shuttle, which is called Buran (Russian for "snowstorm"), made two orbits of the Earth and landed three hours and 25 minutes after the launch.

The Soviet shuttle looks remarkably similar to the United States shuttle, with the same design of delta-shaped wings. But the Soviet shuttle is not fitted with reusable rockets like the American shuttle. Instead these rockets are placed on the Energia booster and the shuttle only has small engines of its own.

TASS, the Soviet press agency, says that the next step is for a launch of a manned shuttle. Several shuttles are being built and there is a space crew ready for Buran.

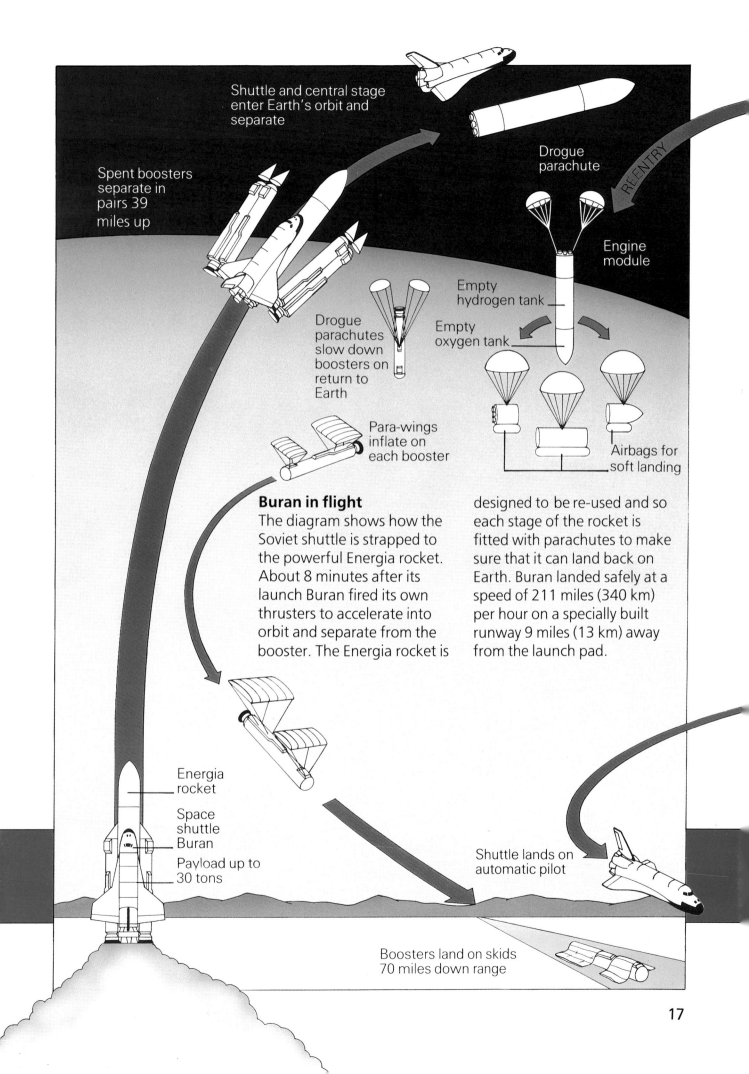

Shuttle and central stage enter Earth's orbit and separate

Drogue parachute

REENTRY

Spent boosters separate in pairs 39 miles up

Engine module

Empty hydrogen tank

Empty oxygen tank

Drogue parachutes slow down boosters on return to Earth

Airbags for soft landing

Para-wings inflate on each booster

Buran in flight

The diagram shows how the Soviet shuttle is strapped to the powerful Energia rocket. About 8 minutes after its launch Buran fired its own thrusters to accelerate into orbit and separate from the booster. The Energia rocket is designed to be re-used and so each stage of the rocket is fitted with parachutes to make sure that it can land back on Earth. Buran landed safely at a speed of 211 miles (340 km) per hour on a specially built runway 9 miles (13 km) away from the launch pad.

Energia rocket

Space shuttle Buran

Payload up to 30 tons

Shuttle lands on automatic pilot

Boosters land on skids 70 miles down range

Soviet space stations

◁ Romanenko, a space
veteran, spent 96 days on
board Salyut 6 in 1977-78,
and 326 days on Mir during 1987.

The Soviet Union is already operating a basic space station. Since February 1986 Mir has been permanently manned, with a series of missions bringing up food, fuel, water, and fresh crews. It has solar panels to provide power and a scientific laboratory, Kvant (Quantum) which was locked onto one of Mir's docking ports. Mir itself consists simply of living accommodation and control equipment. By attaching a series of modules to the six docking ports, it can be turned into a fully-functioning space station. The Russians are also planning an even larger space station, Mir-2, for 1994. Energia will carry the core and modules into space and it is expected that the shuttle will be designed so that it can dock to Mir-2.

The Soviet cosmonauts are pioneering long-term stays in space to provide vital expertise for future shuttle programs. Romanenko stayed in Mir from February to December 1987, a total of 326 days. Romanenko was in good shape after his record-breaking stay – though he had grown half an inch due to weightlessness.

◁ Mir, launched in February 1986, is a simple spacecraft designed to form the first element in a modular space station created by locking separate items on to its six docking ports. By April 1987 the station had four modules and weighed 58 tons. The long solar panels were put in place by the crew on a space walk.

◁ Mir space station is controlled from the nerve center at Kaliningrad.

Destination Mars

The Soviet Union has declared that it wants to land men on Mars by early in the next century – and has offered to collaborate with the US in the venture. A manned trip to Mars would be a massive undertaking, lasting almost three years and costing at least $70 billion. It would stretch the budgets and the knowledge of long-stay manned space travel to the limit, and some believe that it could only be done with space shuttles flying from space stations which would act as staging posts from Earth. Yet we are already fairly certain, based on unmanned expeditions, that Mars has no life. So why do it? The Russians argue that, apart from the Moon, Mars is the only place in the solar system that could possibly be colonized by people.

▽ The Phobos unmanned spacecraft being prepared for launch in 1989.

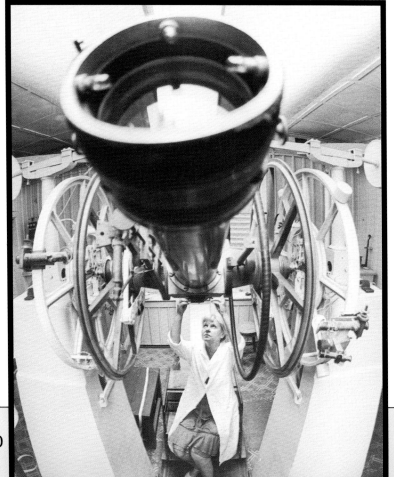

Meanwhile, the Soviet Union has launched two unmanned satellites to Mars, carrying experiments from several countries. The plan includes a landing on a Martian Moon, Phobos.

Soviet and American scientists have already had preliminary discussions on a follow-up mission in 1998, to bring back samples of Martian soil for analysis on Earth. The samples would be picked up by a robot vehicle which might roam around the Martian surface for up to a year. This much is possible; but a manned mission would be at least ten times more expensive, and would depend on continued good relations between the superpowers over many years. The United States has not turned the idea down, but remains noncommittal.

Detailed pictures of the surface of Mars, taken by the United States spacecraft Viking in 1976, show a rock-strewn desert, colored a vivid orange by iron oxides — rust. The sky is pink, caused by tiny dust particles in the thin atmosphere which scatter the sunlight. Often, strong winds whip up huge dust storms lasting months. The two Viking spacecraft, which landed in different places, found a similar terrain but no signs of life.

△ The two Phobos spacecraft, each weighing six tons, were launched by Proton launchers within a few days of one another. All went well until an error by an operator caused contact with one of them to be lost while still on its journey to Mars. The other continues to function well.

Conflict in space

The Soviet shuttle and launcher have one compelling advantage over the American design, which Pentagon analysts have not been slow to grasp. Because the Energia launcher is totally separate from the shuttle, it can be used to launch other things – which might include space "battle stations" designed to attack US satellites or to provide a defense system.

There is no direct evidence that the Soviet Union intends to use Energia in this way. But the Russians have developed a primitive satellite killer, while the US has been engaged since 1983 on a massive program, the Strategic Defense Initiative, (SDI or Star Wars) designed to provide a space-based defense against missiles.

SDI would use lasers, beams of particles or high velocity guns to attack missiles in flight. The system would need to destroy thousands of warheads within a few minutes if it were to provide complete protection for the United States. This is a task that many engineers consider impossible. And deploying it would require changes in the anti-ballistic missile treaty which bans such systems.

Nonetheless, the United States has already spent billions of dollars developing SDI, and there is some evidence that the Soviet Union is working on a similar system. It seems likely that the shuttles and their launchers will play a major part in carrying weapons into space.

▷ Experiments launched into space by rockets like Delta have already demonstrated the ability to destroy satellites by homing in on them and colliding hundreds of miles above the Earth. Techniques like these will be vital to the success of Star Wars.

△ A space-based defense system would first detect enemy missile launches, using a satellite (1). Laser battle stations (2) would attack the missiles in the boost phase, then destroy the "bus" carrying the warheads (3). A further surveillance satellite (4) detects any surviving warheads and decoys, and activates a third defensive layer (5). An infra-red probe in space sends information about any further warheads to ground-based systems (7) which destroy them before they can explode.

▽ Part of an experimental laser in the SDI program.

Sky high: the cost of space travel

Space travel is expensive, so expensive that Western Europe has had to combine resources in the European Space Agency to keep even a toe in the water. In the United States, despite the triumphs of the Apollo Moon landings which cost $24 billion, Congress could not be persuaded to provide money for the next target, Mars. The shuttle was supposed to be built at the same time as the space station it would serve – but to save costs the station was postponed, leaving the shuttle with nowhere to go. Today the emphasis is on cooperation, to spread the costs. Nine nations from ESA, plus Japan and Canada, will help finance the space station. And for a fee of $12 million Britain may accept the invitation to send a cosmonaut to the Soviet Mir space station to carry out experiments.

The bread and butter of space remains the launching of commercial satellites, to carry TV signals or telephone conversations. By the year 2000 this market will be worth $15 billion a year. At present, ESA's Ariane and the United States shuttle compete for contracts, but the Soviet Union has entered the market with its Proton launcher, and the Japanese are also expected to compete before long.

▽ The Soviet Union will launch your satellite, for a fee. Here an Indian satellite is ready for launch on a Soviet rocket at Baikonur Cosmodrome. But the United States government will not allow American firms to buy rides on Soviet rockets.

Global communications today depend on the satellites of Intelsat, an international group to which more than 100 countries belong. These carry phone calls and TV pictures from one side of the Earth to the other, 24 hours a day. The first Intelsat was Early Bird, launched in April 1965. It had one channel that could carry 240 telephone calls and a television circuit. Today Intelsat satellites have 15,000 channels and can carry thousands of telephone calls simultaneously.

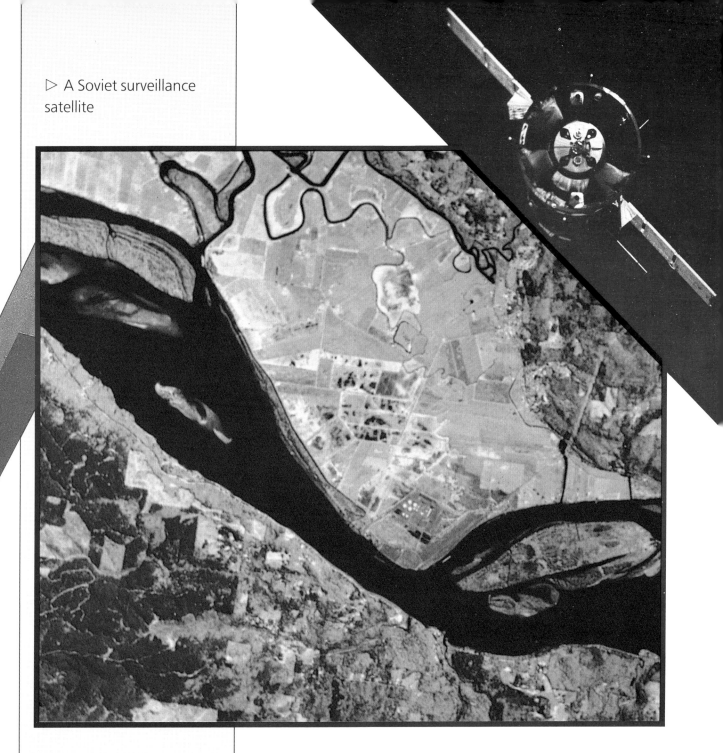

▷ A Soviet surveillance satellite

△ The Soviet Union will now sell its surveillance pictures to anybody who asks. The American and French satellite pictures are also for sale, increasing the competition. This photograph shows an area of Astoria, Oregon, taken by a Soviet satellite.

Manufacturing in space has hardly begun, but according to some estimates it could be worth as much as $40 billion by the year 2000. Drugs, computer chips, alloys and magnetic tape could all be made in space, recovering some of the huge investments made by the two superpowers in space stations.

The advantage of space manufacturing is that in the absence of gravity some processes – including the growth of crystals – work much better than they do on Earth.

Global alternatives

By the 21st century, the United States and the Soviet Union may not have shuttle technology to themselves. The French-designed Hermes, a shuttle about 70 feet long and carrying a crew of two or three and a payload of approximately three tons, is being developed to ride into orbit on top of the Ariane rocket. If ESA declines to finance Hermes, which is expected to cost about $4.25 billion, France will develop it alone.

Japan is also designing a small shuttle, 49 ft long (15m) and with a payload of 1.5 tons, to be carried on its H-2 launcher, perhaps as early as 1995. The same year the Chinese may launch a similar-sized shuttle on an uprated version of their Long March 3 rocket.

West Germany is working on a different concept – a small orbiter called Saenger, carried up into the atmosphere on top of a large launch plane before being released to power its way into orbit with its own rockets. Similar ideas have been developed in the United States. The head start given by being launched at 40,000 feet enables the rocket to carry twice the payload into orbit.

ariane · e · esa
agence spatiale européenne
european space agency

◁ The European rocket Ariane blasts off from the pad. Ariane, the most powerful rocket outside the United States and the Soviet Union, is the main rival to the United States shuttle for commercial space launches.

▷ Hermes is a mini-shuttle intended not for launching satellites but for carrying a two- or three-man crew into orbit.

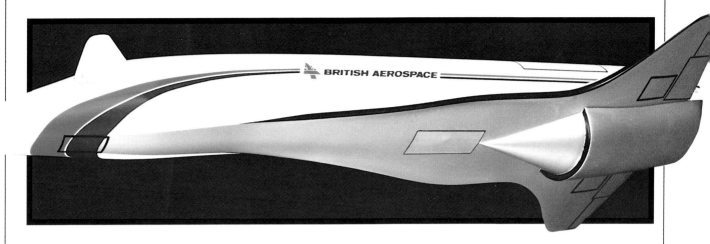

△ HOTOL is a space plane that would be revolutionary if ever built. But it would cost billions of dollars and the British Government has refused to support it. Its future depends on finding finance from some other source willing to invest in a project that will become a reality only after many years of research.

But the most futuristic concept of all is the British HOTOL – horizontal takeoff and landing craft. This spaceplane would take off from a runway using an air-breathing engine. In the thin air of the upper atmosphere a rocket engine would take over and drive HOTOL into orbit. HOTOL could ferry astronauts to a space station, or carry passengers from London to Australia in an hour. Many people believe the future lies in "single stage to orbit" technology like HOTOL.

Japan could well be the third nation to launch its own manned space program. The Japanese shuttle would be used for servicing manned space platforms or for taking people to a Japanese module on the NASA space station.

Leaving the cradle

The Russians have long believed that the Earth is a cradle from which mankind will eventually escape, just as a baby leaves its crib when it learns to crawl. The success of the space station Mir, and the first launch of Buran, are important stages in this process.

But does the future of spaceflight lie with shuttles, rockets, or with completely new technology like HOTOL? So far, the shuttles have yet to prove they have overwhelming advantages over conventional rockets. The American shuttle was designed to make space travel routine, but it is the Russians who have achieved that, using ordinary "throwaway" rockets. While the United States is reluctant to launch unless conditions are perfect, the Russians launch in rain, fog, and even sent off an Indian satellite in March 1988 in a blinding snowstorm.

Eventually the future of space flight may lie with craft like HOTOL, which can get into orbit in a single stage from ordinary runways, then land at airports wherever they choose. Such craft could replace both space launchers and long-distance airliners.

▷ Buran blasted off from Baikonur on 3,000 tons of thrust provided by Energia and four strap-on boosters. After an eight-minute burn Buran reached a height of 60 miles, and a speed of 17,000 miles per hour. At this point Energia separated and Buran went into a low 100 mile orbit by firing its orbital thrusters. After two orbits, it turned tail-first and fired the thrusters again to slow it down for reentry into the atmosphere. Surface temperatures during reentry reached 1,550°C and discolored a few of the heat-resistant tiles which cover the surface of the space shuttle. But Buran, undamaged, landed perfectly (bottom right).

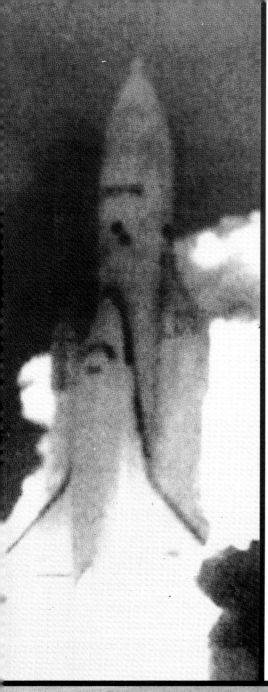

For the moment, single stage to orbit craft like HOTOL are still on the drawing board. The best short-term answer may belong to the Russians – a powerful rocket, Energia, that can launch a shuttle, or be used on its own to launch other payloads. This option gives the Soviets greater flexibility and the ability to launch heavier payloads than the Americans. However, with the successful launch of Discovery and Atlantis there is a new optimism about the U.S. shuttle program.

So far it is the ancient rivalries of nationalism that have provided the spur for space exploration. In future the cost may be too great, or the task too big, for one nation alone. Already the Europeans have united their efforts in space, and even the two superpowers may one day be forced to cooperate instead of competing. A manned landing on Mars some time next century might provide the first opportunity. Until then, the era of the space shuttles will be one of continued competition, as mankind makes use of them to begin the colonization of space.

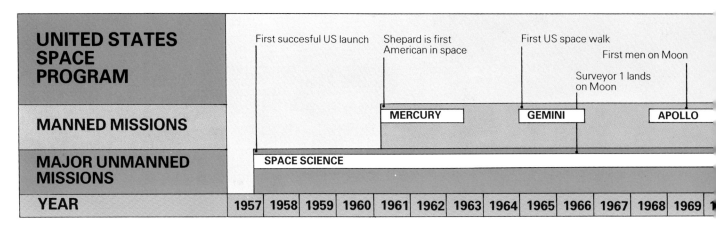

UNITED STATES SPACE PROGRAM												
First succesful US launch · Shepard is first American in space · First US space walk · First men on Moon · Surveyor 1 lands on Moon

| MANNED MISSIONS | MERCURY | GEMINI | APOLLO |

| MAJOR UNMANNED MISSIONS | SPACE SCIENCE |

| YEAR | 1957 | 1958 | 1959 | 1960 | 1961 | 1962 | 1963 | 1964 | 1965 | 1966 | 1967 | 1968 | 1969 |

Shuttle facts

The first shuttle launch took place on April 12, 1981. There was a crew of two – John Young and Robert Crippen. The launch had been delayed by a day for technical reasons, but once off the ground everything went smoothly. Young and Crippen brought the shuttle in to land in California two days later without a hitch. A few of the heat-resistant tiles on the under side of the orbiter had been damaged during the launch, but despite fears, this caused no problems during the descent. The shuttle they flew – Columbia – has since flown six more times with no difficulties.

The US shuttle
A total of five United States shuttles were built. The first, called Enterprise after the spaceship in the TV series Star Trek, never flew in space. It was used for landing tests, then retired to a museum. Challenger, the second shuttle to fly, flew nine times before the disaster that destroyed it. This leaves three shuttles in the active list: Discovery, Columbia and Atlantis.

The Soviet shuttle
The first flight of the Soviet shuttle took place November 15, 1988. The existence of a Soviet shuttle had been rumored for many years, but

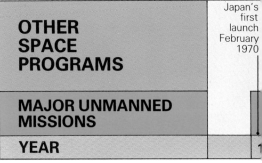

OTHER SPACE PROGRAMS		
Japan's first launch February 1970

| MAJOR UNMANNED MISSIONS | |

| YEAR | |

was not officially confirmed until 1982. Although drawings of the shuttle had been published in Western journals, the first photographs did not appear until September 1988. It is believed that the Soviet Union has built a total of five shuttles.

Shuttle Power
With all five of its engines firing, the United States shuttle generates about 3,000 tons of thrust, enough energy to light the whole State of

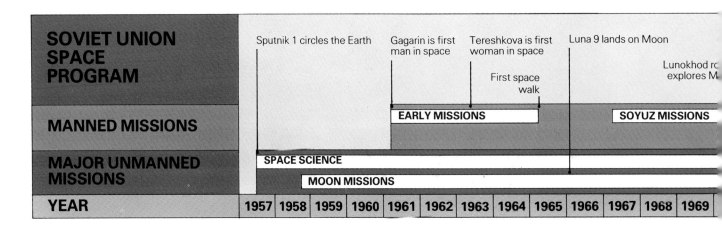

SOVIET UNION SPACE PROGRAM												
Sputnik 1 circles the Earth · Gagarin is first man in space · Tereshkova is first woman in space · First space walk · Luna 9 lands on Moon · Lunokhod ro explores M

| MANNED MISSIONS | EARLY MISSIONS | SOYUZ MISSIONS |

| MAJOR UNMANNED MISSIONS | SPACE SCIENCE / MOON MISSIONS |

| YEAR | 1957 | 1958 | 1959 | 1960 | 1961 | 1962 | 1963 | 1964 | 1965 | 1966 | 1967 | 1968 | 1969 |

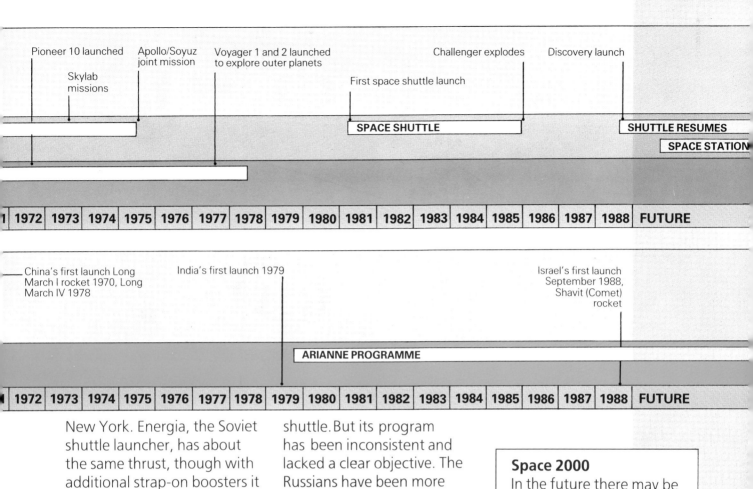

| | 1972 | 1973 | 1974 | 1975 | 1976 | 1977 | 1978 | 1979 | 1980 | 1981 | 1982 | 1983 | 1984 | 1985 | 1986 | 1987 | 1988 | FUTURE |

Pioneer 10 launched

Skylab missions

Apollo/Soyuz joint mission

Voyager 1 and 2 launched to explore outer planets

First space shuttle launch

Challenger explodes

Discovery launch

SPACE SHUTTLE

SHUTTLE RESUMES

SPACE STATION

China's first launch Long March I rocket 1970, Long March IV 1978

India's first launch 1979

Israel's first launch September 1988, Shavit (Comet) rocket

ARIANNE PROGRAMME

| | 1972 | 1973 | 1974 | 1975 | 1976 | 1977 | 1978 | 1979 | 1980 | 1981 | 1982 | 1983 | 1984 | 1985 | 1986 | 1987 | 1988 | FUTURE |

New York. Energia, the Soviet shuttle launcher, has about the same thrust, though with additional strap-on boosters it might generate considerably more. The payload of both shuttles is around 30 tons; but Energia on its own can launch at least 100 tons and possibly up to 230 tons.

Life in Space
The United States won the race to put a man on the Moon, and was first to launch a space shuttle. But its program has been inconsistent and lacked a clear objective. The Russians have been more plodding but more persistent. Their goal has been to make living and working in space routine. By 1988, Soviet cosmonauts had spent over 4,280 days in space, against only 1,621 for the Americans. During 1987 the Soviet Union launched 95 spacecraft, against only eight by the United States.

Space 2000
In the future there may be many more shuttles flying: Japanese, French, Chinese and maybe others not yet thought of. People will use them as a first step in the exploration of the Solar System. They will be the workhorses of space travel, carrying astronauts and materials to and from the lonely emptiness of space.

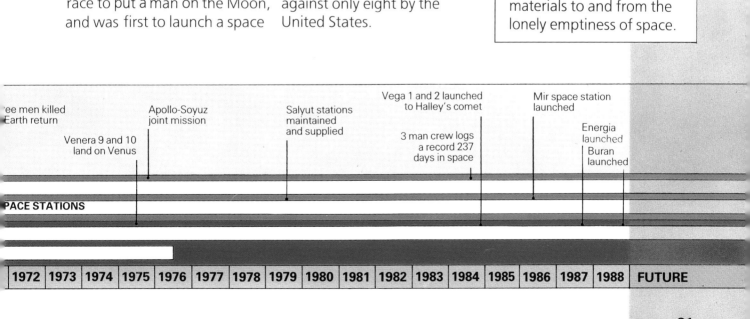

Three men killed Earth return

Venera 9 and 10 land on Venus

Apollo-Soyuz joint mission

Salyut stations maintained and supplied

Vega 1 and 2 launched to Halley's comet

3 man crew logs a record 237 days in space

Mir space station launched

Energia launched

Buran launched

SPACE STATIONS

| 1972 | 1973 | 1974 | 1975 | 1976 | 1977 | 1978 | 1979 | 1980 | 1981 | 1982 | 1983 | 1984 | 1985 | 1986 | 1987 | 1988 | FUTURE |

Index

Photographic credits:

Cover and pages 10, 23, 29 and back cover: Rex Features; pages 4-5, 6-7, 8-9, 12, 19 and 22-23: Associated Press Colour Library; pages 6, 13 (bottom) and 20-21: NASA; pages 8 and 25 (top right): Topham Picture Library; pages 11 (both), 13 (top), 15 and 21: Frank Spooner Agency; pages 16, 17 and 28-29: Associated Press B/W Library; pages 18, 18-19, 20 and 24: TASS News Agency; page 25: Soyuzkarta/ Aerospace America; page 26 (both): European Space Agency; page 27 (top): British Aerospace; page 27 (bottom): Aerospatiale.

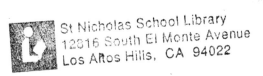